How Not to be Eaten

Written by Rob Alcraft

Contents

Don't get eaten 2
Look out 4
Hide 6
Be quick 8
Stay protected 10
Be smart 12
Be unpleasant 14
Fight back 16
Self-destruct! 18
Still here? 20
Top tips 22

Collins

Don't get eaten

If you are cute and bite-sized, you need to take care!

Here are some top tips to help you stay alive.

Look out

Always stay aware – you must spot predators first.

Keep a lookout.

Stay alert.

Sniff out predators creeping near.

Hide

Don't be detected. You will be
eaten if you are seen. Blend in like a leaf
insect, with your skin, scales, feathers or fur.

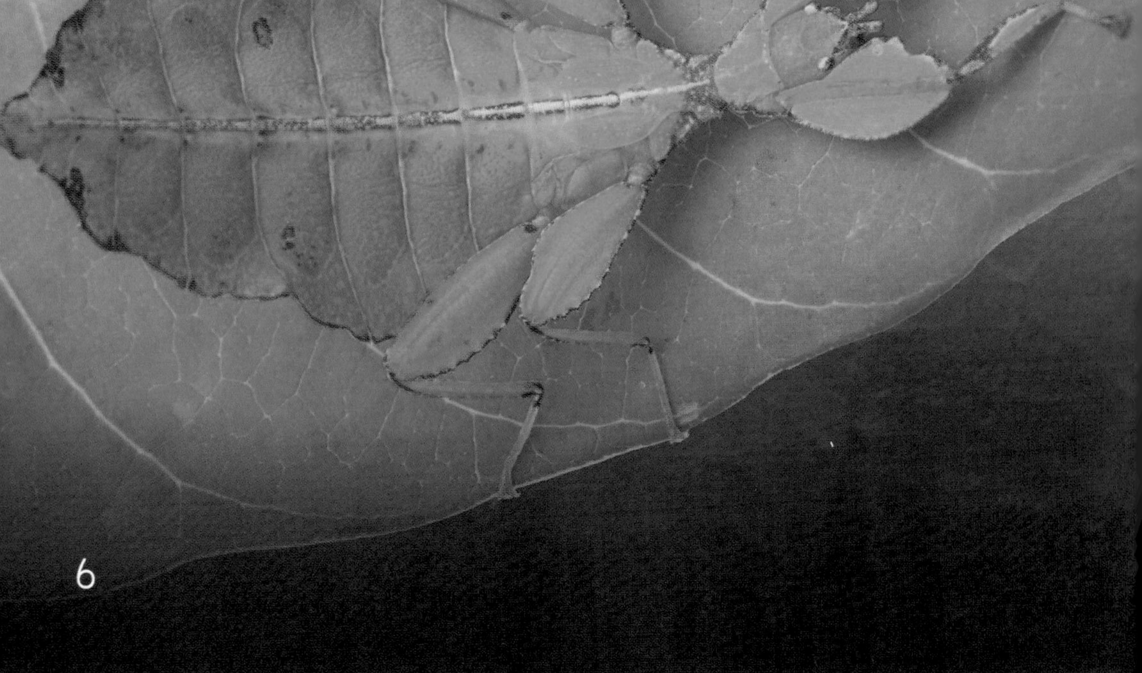

skin
scales
fur
feathers

Be quick

Speed could help you to escape your predators.

Sprint on powerful legs.

Dash away like an antelope.

Zoom as fast as an insect.

Stay protected

Protect your soft bits, and make yourself hard to eat.

Keep safe with sharp quills.

A hard shell can prevent bites.

Thick scales could shield you.

Be smart

Trick predators into leaving you alone.

Bold markings look threatening.

Vanish in a
cloud of ink!

Play dead to be left alone.

Be unpleasant

No predator wants food that is disgusting!

Shoot out
foul-smelling spray.

Make predators gag
on slime.

Fight back

Make predators back off: put up a fight.

Fight as a team – and win.

Spit toxic venom.

Shoot a stinging spray.

Self-destruct!

Never surrender. Discard bits of yourself if you have to.

Let your arms drop off – just get away.

Spew out
your insides!

The lizard escaped –
so could you.

Still here?

You made it – hooray!
Stay on your toes and
keep alert. Don't be eaten!

Top tips

Stay aware ☑

Don't be detected ☑

Be quick ☑

Make yourself hard to eat ☑

Trick predators

Be unpleasant 

Put up a fight

Self-destruct

After reading

Letters and Sounds: Phase 5

Word count: 235

Focus phonemes: /ee/ ea, ie, /e/ ea, /ai/ ay, a-e, /igh/ i-e, /oo/ u-e, ew, ou, /oa/ o, o-e, /or/ al, our /o/ a, /ow/ ou, /u/ o-e, /ar/ a, /air/ are /oo/ oul, /ur/ ir

Common exception words: of, to, the, into, put, are, be, have, so

Curriculum links: Science: Animals

National Curriculum learning objectives: Spoken language: listen and respond appropriately to adults and their peers; Reading/Word reading: apply phonic knowledge and skills as the route to decode words, read accurately by blending sounds in unfamiliar words containing GPCs that have been taught, read common exception words, read other words of more than one syllable that contain taught GPCs, read aloud accurately books that are consistent with their developing phonic knowledge; Reading/Comprehension: understand both the books they can already read accurately and fluently ... by: drawing on what they already know or on background information and vocabulary provided by the teacher

Developing fluency

- Your child may enjoy hearing you read the book.
- You may wish to read the book together, with you reading the main text on each page and your child reading the text in the yellow boxes.

Phonic practice

- Read pages 10–11 to your child. Ask your child:
  - Can you find three words that have the same sound? (e.g. *eat*, *shield*, *keep*)
  - For each word, can you point to the part of the word that represents the /ee/ sound?
  - Practise sounding out the words and then quickly blending the sounds together.
  - Can you think of other words that contain the /ee/ sound? (e.g. *feet*, *teeth*, *meat*)

Extending vocabulary

- Flick through the book together. Talk to your child about the animals. Can they name any? (e.g. *mouse*, *ostrich*, *deer*, *hare*, *fox*, *crab*, *porcupine*)
- Ask your child if they can spot the synonyms below. Can they spot the odd one out?
  - shield run protect (*run*)
  - smart vanish disappear (*smart*)
  - threatening scary play (*play*)